Would
YOU RATHER ?

strictly reserved for teens from 12 to 17 years old

Discover our Activity Book for Teens featuring Word Search, Mandalas, Mazes and Sudoku : "OMG I'm So Bored !"

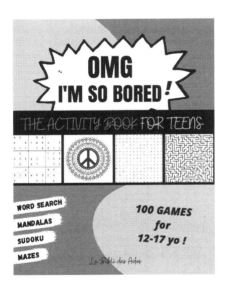

Scan the QR code to find our book on Amazon (UK store) :

Would you Rather

carry a flip phone

OR

only use a desktop computer

never play video games again

OR

never use your favorite
mobile app again

Would you rather

have to listen only
Justin Bieber

OR

only Ariana Grande for the
rest of your life

be a famous rapper

OR

a famous singer

Would you Rather

have to switch closets
with your dad

OR

only wear the clothes your
grandma buys for you

have a famous family member

OR

be the famous family member

Would you Rather

never wear deodorant

OR

have really bad dandruff

wear winter clothes
all year long

OR

summer clothes all year long

Would you Rather

teach a class in high school

OR

have your parents teach one
of your classes

go to school four days a week
for 10 hours

OR

five days a week
for eight hours

Would you rather

eat spicy wings

OR

bite into ice cream

eat your favorite meal
every day

OR

never eat it again

Would you Rather

break everything you touch

OR

get shocked every time
you touch something

live 100 years in the future

OR

100 years in the past

Would you rather

have ten kids

OR

no kids at all

go to your dream college and
have a lot of debt

OR

an okay college and
have no debt

Would you rather

work at a summer camp

OR

lifeguard at a pool

never lose a sports game

OR

never lose an argument

Would you Rather

go on a double date with
your parents

OR

with your significant
other's parents

always smell bad around
the person you like

OR

always say something embarrassing
around the person you like

Would you Rather

spend a day without
your phone

OR

a day with no people at all

only use email to communicate

OR

only use voice calls
(no video calls)

Would you rather

be a famous songwriter

OR

a famous drummer

win American Idol

OR

American Ninja Warrior

Would you rather

have your own family reality TV show

OR

have your own family band

the oldest child

OR

the youngest child

Would you rather

cover yourself in peanut butter

OR

ketchup

only use dog shampoo

OR

never cut your toenails

Would you Rather

sing in front of
the whole school

OR

be in a spelling bee in front of
the entire school

clean the bathrooms at
your school

OR

clean up after lunch in the
cafeteria at your school

Would you rather

have to eat one dog treat per day plus whatever food you want

OR

never eat dog food, but you can only eat cereal

eat steak for a week

OR

ice cream for a week

Would you rather

have super strength

OR

super hearing

make the best movie ever

OR

the best album ever

Would you rather

die peacefully at 60

OR

painfully at 100

be a surgeon

OR

be a college professor

Would you rather

always be first in the school lunch line

OR

always be first out of the school parking lot

be president of your student council

OR

the most popular person in school

Would you rather

date someone who's gorgeous
but unfunny

OR

someone who's okay-looking
but hilarious

date someone three feet
taller than you

OR

three feet shorter than you

Would you rather

have no air conditioning

OR

no heating

only charge your phone once a week

OR

not have a camera on your phone

Would you rather

tour with a famous band

OR

tour with a famous comedian

perform at the Super Bowl
halftime show

OR

play football in the Super Bowl

Would you rather

own a restaurant with your family

OR

own a retail clothing store with your family

have to do laundry for your family

OR

cook meals for your family

Would you rather

eat moldy bread

OR

moldy cheese

have your dog kiss you

OR

your grandma kiss you

Would you Rather

have access to the teacher's lounge

OR

be able to drive a school bus

say the morning announcements

OR

be the school sports commentator

Would you rather

do all the grocery shopping for your family

OR

do all the cooking for your family

never eat condiments again

OR

put them on everything you eat

Would you rather

only be an Instagram
influencer

OR

only be YouTube famous

have a pet dragon

OR

a pet unicorn

Would you Rather

take every vacation to
Disney World

OR

New York City

always have the newest
technology

OR

the best food in the world

Would you rather

eat out by yourself

OR

eat at home with your family

take care of all your family's pets
OR
have no pets at all

Would you rather

have terrible gas all the time

OR

burp out loud constantly

eat a rotten banana

OR

a rotten egg

Would you rather

be allergic to chocolate

OR

allergic to bread

have all your food be spicy

OR

have all your food be sweet

Would you rather

be the richest person in the world and hate what you do

OR

have an average wage and love what you do

read minds

OR

have read every book in the world

Would you rather

have a mansion

OR

a private jet

work for your parents

OR

teach at your high school

Would you Rather

always have the hiccups

OR

always have big sweat stains
under your arms

sniff expired milk

OR

sniff rotten eggs

Would you rather

have a babysitter

OR

be forced to babysit

have really large feet

OR

really large hands

would you rather

lose 10 friends

OR

gain 1 enemie

have a weird smile

OR

a weird laugh

Would you Rather

have a dog that talks

OR

a monkey that dances

have all your teeth fall out

OR

all your hair fall out

Would you rather

have your head attached
backward

OR

your eyes at the back of
your head

kiss a frog

OR

hug a skunk

Would you Rather

swallow gum accidentally

OR

have it stuck in your hair

your younger sister did your homework

OR

you did your younger sister's homework

Would you Rather

have really bushy eyebrows

OR

no eyebrows at all

have a friend that smells weird

OR

a friend that acts weird

Would you rather

your dog pooped on your homework

OR

your dog ate your homework

pour your lunch on the principal

OR

the most popular person in school

Would you Rather

have a big head

OR

a long neck

be caught singing in the bathroom loudly

OR

talking to yourself in the mirror

Would you rather

be a terrible dancer

OR

be a terrible singer

have an embarrassing picture of you circulate around school

OR

circulate on the internet

Would you Rather

your mom dressed funny to school

OR

brought your baby pictures to show your classmates

have parents who dress like teenagers

OR

parents who dress like grandparents

Would you Rather

not be able to hear anything
while watching TV

OR

not be able to see anything

have to wear a clown nose

OR

a clown wig everywhere you go

Would you rather

find out Santa Claus was real

OR

Tooth Fairies were real

always laugh at sad things

OR

always cry at funny things

Would you rather

fall asleep on a public bus

OR

in class

eat the family pet

OR

not eat for a week

Would you Rather

use someone else's toothbrush

OR

find out someone used your toothbrush

have your face painted while you were asleep

OR

have your tummy painted

Would you rather

wake up with a new face

OR

wake up to see a new family

meet a mini you

OR

an evil version of you

would you rather

prank your neighbor

OR

stalk your neighbor

wear oversized clothes to school

OR

clothes that are much too small

Would you Rather

fall asleep for a year

OR

have insomnia for a year

have gap teeth

OR

have to use braces for your teeth

Would you rather

have six fingers

OR

six toes

be trapped in a room full of talking dolls

OR

walking teddy bears

Would you Rather

your mom kiss your cheeks in public

OR

call you your childhood nickname in public

be so tired your mom had to bath you

OR

be so tired your best friend had to bath you

Would you rather

wake up to find your hair bald

OR

to find out that your hair
turned pink

your friend uploaded a picture
where your outfit looked weird

OR

your face looked weird

Would you rather

your best friend dressed like someone from the 80's

OR

someone from another planet entirely

be dumped in front of the whole school

OR

be dumped on a live video online

Would you Rather

chase a crawling cockroach

OR

be chased by a flying cockroach

have a childish older sibling

OR

a younger sibling that likes to boss you around

Would you Rather

be known as the teacher's pet in school

OR

be known as mummy's pet at home

snore when you sleep

OR

talk when you sleep

Would you Rather

have to work on a farm after school

OR

have to work on a field after school

share your room with your sibling

OR

move into the attic

Would you rather

have your phone taken away

OR

your laptop taken away

it was winter all the time

OR

it was summer all the time

Would you Rather

have a pool

OR

a jacuzzi

act as the villain in a movie

OR

be the hero

Would you Rather

meet a famous movie star

OR

famous musician

be able to walk through doors

OR

be able to teleport

Would you Rather

get dumped via text message

OR

in front of all your friends

take a group picture with your friends

OR

a group selfie

Would you Rather

take a shower

OR

take a bath

be an adult already

OR

be a child again

Would you Rather

work part-time at a clothing store

OR

a bookstore

be alone when sick

OR

have a lot of friends around

Would you Rather

be at the top of your class academically

OR

top of your team in sports

eat in bed

OR

in front of the TV

Would you rather

eat a bowl of ice-cream

OR

drink a cup of hot chocolate

watch a reality show

OR

be on a reality show

Would you Rather

ride on a horse's back

OR

a camel's back

eat only vegetables for
a month

OR

eat only fruits for a month

would you rather

know how to play the piano

OR

know how to play the guitar

have a lot of money

OR

be good looking

Would you rather

have a best friend who's an introvert

OR

one who's an extrovert

be in a relationship with someone far away

OR

someone in your class

Would you Rather

your parents adopted another child

OR

find out you were adopted

be in a hurry and have to skip breakfast

OR

be too tired and have to skip dinner

Would you rather

testify against your sibling

OR

go to a juvenile center

only use your phone for five minutes a day for a month

OR

go without your phone for three months

Would you Rather

someone read your diary

OR

someone read your messages

cheat on a test

OR

fail a test

Would you Rather

watch your crush get
embarrassed in public

OR

be embarrassed in the
presence of your crush

delete Snap

OR

stop watching Insta
stories

Would you Rather

have nosy parents

OR

strict parents

be the best player on a
losing team

OR

the worst player on a
winning team

Would you Rather

lie to your crush

OR

lie to your best friend

be home alone after school

OR

be with a very annoying relative

Would you rather

be in a crowded room at night

OR

be in a dark room all alone at night

be popular but have fake friends

OR

be unpopular but have real friends

Would you rather

break your crush's heart

OR

have your crush break your heart

drop your phone into water accidentally

OR

drop your mom's phone into water accidentally

Would you rather

give up on junks forever

OR

give up on meat forever

be a teen parent

OR

never have a child again

Would you rather

your tongue gets longer
every time you lie

OR

gets shorter every time you
say something insulting

stay in a coma for 15 years

OR

be in prison for 15 years

Would you rather

live with just your dad

OR

live with just your mom

get married at 20

OR

get married at 60

Would you Rather

misplace 100 dollars

OR

give 1000 dollars to charity

do all the cleaning at home

OR

all the cooking

Would you Rather

live in a cave

OR

on an island

your Instagram account got hacked

OR

you forgot the password to your Instagram account

Would you rather

be kicked out of a sports team

OR

be forced to withdraw from a sports team

fail a test you read really hard for

OR

fall sick and be unable to sit for the test

Would you rather

lick grandma's feet

OR

tickle her feet with your tongue

lick your socks

OR

lick the sole of your shoe

Would you Rather

have meat stuck in between
your teeth

OR

fish bone stuck in between
your teeth

let worms crawl up your nose

OR

crawl into your ears

Would you rather

look like a dog

OR

smell like a dog

eat a bar of soap

OR

drink liquid soap

Would you Rather

lick a maggot

OR

swallow a worm

forget to shower to school

OR

forget to wear underwear

Would you Rather

drink a gallon of mayonnaise

OR

gallon of mustard

eat food from the floor

OR

lick ice-cream from the floor

Would you rather

sniff your armpit in public

OR

scratch your butt

sneeze into your food

OR

into your crush's food

Would you Rather

have noodles for hair

OR

worms for hair

be served food on a dirty plate

OR

be served dirty food

Would you rather

have a spider crawl in your hair

OR

crawl on your face

sleep on a bed sheet that smelled of poop

OR

a bedsheet that has poop stains

Would you rather

wash the really dirty toilet

OR

place your butt on a really dirty toilet seat

Get a full time job

OR

go to college

Would you rather

live in Narnia

OR

go to school at Hogwarts

save your country from an invasion

OR

from a terrible disease

Would you Rather

all of the members of the opposite sex liked you

OR

have the prettiest (but dumb) girl in school as a girlfriend

eat a small can of dog food

OR

six overripe bananas

Would you Rather

have to eat a bowl full of worms

OR

a live frog

lose your ability to speak

OR

have to say everything you are thinking

Would you rather

have to listen to music all of the time

OR

not be able to listen to music at all

have live one hundred years in the future

OR

one hundred years in the past

Would you Rather

live an extra 25 years

OR

live a life without the need to sleep

have slow but unlimited Internet

OR

paid but limited Internet

Would you rather

be able to read minds

OR

to predict the future

look 10 years older from the
neck up

OR

the neck down

Would you rather

have 20 million YT subscribers

OR

produce a blockbuster action movie

kill one human being

OR

50 baby animals

Would you Rather

only use TikTok for the rest of
your life

OR

only use YT for the rest
of your life

know how you die

OR

when you die

Printed in Great Britain
by Amazon